THEN & NOW

CODY

OPPOSITE: Cody was founded in 1896 and incorporated in 1901. Looking towards the northwest, with the Absaroka Range of the Rocky Mountains in the distance, the town is shown about 1903 or 1904. The Irma Hotel is the two-story building in the background, and the Cody Canal, which brought water from the Southfork of the Shoshone River for the town's residents, is in the foreground. (Sturm/ Lovelace collection.)

THEN & NOW

CODY

Lynn Johnson Houze

To the past and present photographers of Cody, who made this book possible

Copyright © 2011 by Lynn Johnson Houze
ISBN 978-0-7385-7425-7

Library of Congress Control Number: 2010934811

Published by Arcadia Publishing
Charleston, South Carolina

Printed in the United States of America

For all general information, please contact Arcadia Publishing:
Telephone 843-853-2070
Fax 843-853-0044
E-mail sales@arcadiapublishing.com
For customer service and orders:
Toll-Free 1-888-313-2665

Visit us on the Internet at www.arcadiapublishing.com

ON THE FRONT COVER: The Irma Hotel was built by Col. William F. "Buffalo Bill" Cody and named for his youngest daughter. The gala opening on November 18, 1902, was attended by over 500 people—more than the town's population. The colonel announced the engagement of Irma to Lt. Clarence Stott that evening, adding to the excitement. At the time of its opening, the Irma was considered to be the most modern hotel in the Rocky Mountain region, having cost $80,000 to build. The Irma continues to be the most prominent and historical landmark in town. (Now image, Jennifer Houze.)

ON THE BACK COVER: Sheridan Avenue, Cody's main street, runs east to west. The streets in the original part of town were laid out wider than usual as a precaution against fire spreading from one side of the street to the other. The C made up of whitewashed rocks in the distance was first put on Rattlesnake Mountain in 1927 by the Cody High School senior class. Annually, in August, the current senior class repaints the rocks and adds their class year to the middle of the C.

CONTENTS

ACKNOWLEDGMENTS

I have had a great deal of enjoyment in discovering new and previously unpublished photographs for use in this book. It has also been wonderful reconnecting with old friends: those images that I've used before and those that are iconic in Cody photographic history. The support that I received from private individuals, institutions, collectors, and local historians in locating images has been overwhelming. I feel very fortunate for the assistance that I received, and it has been a pleasure to work with these people throughout the project.

First and foremost, I want to thank my daughter, Jennifer Houze, for all of her excellent photography work; I couldn't have done this book without her. Altamae Markham read my manuscript and helped me with locations of places and businesses that came and went long before I came to Cody. Ester Johansson-Murray, who has always encouraged me in my writing, answered all my questions, no matter how strange or unusual they were. They both have been wonderful, and I truly appreciate their help and friendship.

Pete Lovelace kindly gave me total access to his Harold Sturm photograph collection and allowed me to choose whatever images I wanted. It was a great experience. Many thanks go to Chris Gimmeson, Mack Frost, and Sean Campbell at the Buffalo Bill Historical Center (BBHC) for their photographic help. They have been terrific, and I appreciate it very much. Marylin Schultz and Lyn Stallings at the Park County Archives were of tremendous help in finding and scanning the photographs that I requested. Mary Robinson and the staff of the McCracken Research Library at the BBHC, Cindy Brown at the Wyoming State Archives in Cheyenne, and John Waggener and the staff at the American Heritage Center at the University of Wyoming, Laramie, also aided me in procuring Cody images. And thanks also to Jeremy Johnston, managing editor of the *Papers of William F. Cody* and fellow Arcadia author, for his encouragement. Thank you to the individuals who allowed me to use their family photographs, many of which have not been published before: Nancy and Dave Wulfing, Bob Landgren, Marge and Dick Wilder, Len Pearson, Fran Swope, Dale and Bill Delph, and Paul James. Special thanks goes to Lee Hermann, who took the aerial photograph on page 76 from the exact perspective and angle that I wanted.

I also want to thank the Wyoming State Historical Society for awarding me a Lola Homsher Grant to help with my expenses. Their financial assistance is greatly appreciated.

Finally, I would like to thank those local authors before me for all the work they've done over the years in recording the history of Cody. Again, as with my previous book, I want to say a special thank you to two of them: Beryl Churchill, for her work dealing with the Buffalo Bill Dam and the irrigation systems, and Ester Johansson-Murray, for her book on the North Fork. Their books were invaluable to me.

In the interest of brevity, abbreviations will be used for the following three image sources in the courtesy lines: Park County Archives (Cody, Wyoming), PCA; Buffalo Bill Historical Center (Cody, Wyoming), BBHC; Harold Sturm photographs from Pete Lovelace's collection (Cody, Wyoming), Sturm/Lovelace. Unless otherwise noted, all images are from the author's collection.

INTRODUCTION

Cody, Wyoming, is located in an area of northwest Wyoming known as the Big Horn Basin. The basin is surrounded by mountain ranges on three sides: the Absaroka Range to the west, the Owl Mountains located to the south, and the Big Horn Mountains to the east. Yellowstone National Park, which was founded in 1872 as the first U.S. national park, is located almost 53 miles to the west of Cody. The Big Horn Basin was restricted from white settlement by treaties with the American Indians in 1868. Ten years later, those restrictions were lifted, and early settlers slowly began to enter the basin. Therefore, this area was one of the last frontiers within the lower 48 states, if not the last, to be settled. By 1890, Wyoming had achieved statehood, and more people began to homestead here, though even now Wyoming is the least populated of all 50 states.

William F. "Buffalo Bill" Cody was visiting Sheridan, Wyoming, in 1894 when his son-in-law Horace Boal gave him a close look at this area from the top eastern side of the Big Horn Mountains. While Cody had heard of this area from Indians, Yale paleontologist O. C. Marsh, and others, he had never been to the northern basin. A group of Sheridan businessmen were already interested in founding a town here, and Cody eagerly joined the effort. He saw the beauty of the region, its proximity to Yellowstone National Park (which was already attracting tourists), the abundance of game and fish, and the available land for ranching and farming. The only major element missing was sufficient water to enable ranchers and farmers to make a living off the land, as this is high desert country. The Shoshone River, previously named Stinking Water by the Crow Indians, did run through this area, however, which meant there was potential for bringing more water to the land.

By 1895, the Shoshone Land and Irrigation Company was founded and made up of George T. Beck, William F. Cody, Nate Salsbury, Harry Gerrans, Bronson Rumsey, Horace Alger, and George Bleistein. That year, an initial town site was laid out near DeMaris Hot Springs, two miles west of present-day Cody. Beck did not like the location or the fact that a great deal of the land was already owned by Charles DeMaris, for whom the Hot Springs are named. And DeMaris was not interested in selling the land either. Beck began looking at other possibilities a little to the east and soon settled on the town's present location. In the fall of 1895, work began on the Cody Canal, which would carry water from the Southfork of the Shoshone River northeast to the town. In May 1896, Beck and surveyor Charles Hayden laid out the town at its present location.

"The colonel," as the townspeople often referred to William F. Cody in those early years, invested a great deal of money in the birth and growth of the town. George Beck was the town founder who lived here and oversaw its ups and downs. The Chicago, Burlington and Quincy Railroad headquartered in Lincoln, Nebraska, was interested in building a spur line to Cody from Toluca, Montana, which ran from Billings, Montana, to southern Wyoming. In order to make sure that the railroad did build that line all the way to Cody, the Shoshone Land and Irrigation Company sold the majority of the town lots to the railroad company. As a result, the railroad had a vested interest in the success of the town, as it would be making money from the sale of the lots. Additionally, the Shoshone Irrigation Company dropped the word "Land" from its company name.

An attempt at publishing a newspaper called the *Shoshone Valley News* was made in 1896, but it only lasted a short while. The first edition of the *Cody Enterprise* was published in August 1899 and is still publishing today. It has gone through several name changes over the years, but to this day the masthead honors Buffalo Bill as its founder. By 1900, the town had a population of just over 300, and in 1901 Cody was incorporated. That same year marked the completion of the Chicago, Burlington and Quincy Railroad line from Toluca to the Cody Depot, which was located on the north side of the Shoshone River.

Before Cody's founding in 1896, the community of Marquette was already established near the confluence of the south and north branches of the Shoshone River, located west of the canyon formed by the river between Rattlesnake and Cedar Mountains. It had a general store, school, several saloons, and a number of ranches. The confluence is about eight miles west of the town of Cody and was seen as the logical place to construct a dam, thereby creating a reservoir to supply water to the western part of the Big Horn Basin. In 1902, the Newlands Reclamation Act decreed that all funds received by the federal government from the disposition and sale of public lands in the 16 Western states were to be used to construct dam and irrigation systems that were too large and too costly to be undertaken by the private sector. The Shoshone River Valley Project was the first project undertaken after the passage of this act. Cody assigned his water rights to the Reclamation Service in 1904, and work building and improving the road between Cody and the dam site began that spring. The construction of the dam meant that the area known as Marquette would be flooded, necessitating either the removal or the abandonment of the ranches and the buildings there. In 1946, to commemorate Buffalo Bill's 100th birthday, the dam and the reservoir were renamed after him.

Today Cody is a popular tourist stop on the way to and from Yellowstone, which is just as William F. Cody envisioned it. It also is a hunter's and fisherman's paradise, and irrigation has overcome the high desert climate, enabling ranchers and farmers to be successful. The population and the area have grown, sometimes in "fits and spurts," as detailed in the pages that follow.

CHAPTER 1

THE ORIGINAL TOWN

William F. "Buffalo Bill" Cody founded the *Cody Enterprise* in August 1899. The office was located on the north side of Sheridan Avenue between Sixteenth and Seventeenth Streets. Col. J. H. Peake, a newspaperman from Washington, D.C., was brought to Cody by Buffalo Bill to be the editor. Anna "Granny" Peake, shown here, ran the paper after his untimely death in 1905. (PCA, 00-06-46.)

The town was still sparsely settled when this house was photographed in the fall of 1902. Situated on the corner of Alger Avenue and Seventeenth Street, also known as the "Greybull Hill" because the road leads to the town of Greybull, the updated house is now the Bargain Box, a resale shop owned by the Christ Episcopal Church. (Then image, BBHC, P.5.1598; now image, author.)

The first rodeo grounds were located west of town where the Buffalo Bill Historical Center is today. Tommy Trimmer is shown competing in a Fourth of July stakes race in 1907 with the town's "Little Red School" in the background. Today the Cody High School complex and its football field occupy all the land seen in the vicinity of that school. (Then image, PCA, 00-06-91; now image, author.)

A fire occurred in November 1908 on the southwest corner of Sheridan Avenue and Thirteenth Street in the center of town. Caused by high wind, the blaze destroyed several businesses but did not cross the street to the north. The men on the telephone pole are working to repair the lines. (Then image, PCA, P80-12-083; now image, author.)

Since the early days of Cody, parades along Sheridan Avenue have been held not only to celebrate the Fourth of July but also for special occasions, including Buffalo Bill's return to Cody at the close of another Wild West season. Even though there were plenty of marchers—including townsfolk, cowboys from area ranches, and American Indians from reservations in Montana, among others—there were always many spectators, as people from around the Big Horn Basin came to Cody for the parades. Originally the parade route was east to west, but for many years now, it runs west to east. (Then image, BBHC, P.6.781; now image, author.)

THE ORIGINAL TOWN

By 1912, businesses were beginning to fill up the lots on the north side of Sheridan Avenue across from the Irma Hotel, which is off to the right. Twelfth Street on the far, or east, side of the Irma was then the town's main street. It went north through town and across the Shoshone River to the railroad depot. (Now image, Jennifer Houze.)

THE ORIGINAL TOWN

Howard Brundage built Brundage Hardware Company in 1898 on the north side of Sheridan Avenue. Seen here in 1912, it was one of the first buildings between Eleventh and Twelfth Streets and housed a second business that was owned by Richard Roth. The hardware store also had a shooting range in the basement. (Then image, PCA, 86-024-040; now image, author.)

The Scarf Building was erected in 1905 and contained a combination jewelry and drugstore on the first floor, with Dr. Bennett's office on the second floor. It is located at the intersection of Sheridan Avenue and Twelfth Street, known then as the "Four Corners" because the buildings' front doors faced each other diagonally. (Then image, PCA, 94-26-04; now image, author.)

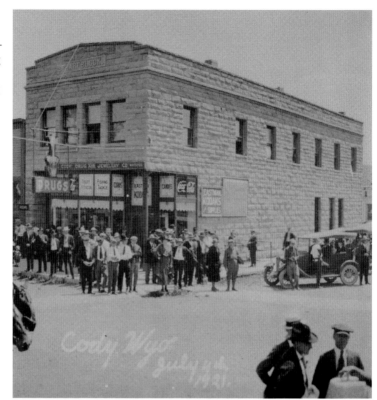

Cody Trading Company was founded in 1898 by Jakie Schwoob, one of the town's founders, and was the successor to the Forbes Trading Company, the first real general store in Cody. This wooden building burned in 1913 but was soon replaced by a larger brick store. Schwoob's motto was "We Sell Everything," and the company did. Cody's oldest business continued at the spot until 1963. Woolworth's opened a store here two years later, remaining there for 25 years. (Then image, PCA, P09-78-20; now image, author.)

Located on the southwest corner of Sixteenth Street and Beck Avenue, this was home for Dolly Trimmer and her son Tommy for several years after they moved to town from Marquette in 1910. The construction of Shoshone Dam and the subsequent flooding of the land between the two branches of the Shoshone River made the move necessary. Later they moved to a house on the south side of Alger Avenue. (Then image, Nancy Trimmer Wulfing collection; now image, author.)

Ranchers and farmers often boarded their horses at the Keystone Barn on Beck Avenue or one of the other liveries when they came to town for supplies. The trip from their homes out on the Southfork to town could take two days. On the front of the building is a 1910 poster for Buffalo Bill's Wild West, announcing its visit to Billings, Montana, the closest to Cody that the exhibition appeared. Today the Cody Convention Center, historically referred to as Cody Auditorium, hosts a variety of events, including craft shows, auctions, parties, and benefits. (Then image, PCA, P95-18-142; now image, author.)

William F. Cody built this house for his older sister Julia Cody Goodman and her family in 1905 for $4,500. It was on the south side of Beck Avenue across the street from the house built for Irma Hotel employees and to the east of the former American Legion Hall. An office building currently occupies the building on the left (modern photograph). Later, when William F. Cody's wife, Louisa, moved to Cody, she lived in the Irma Hotel employee's house. (Then image, BBHC, P.6.527; now image, author.)

Unpaved streets and incandescent streetlights throughout the town were the norm in 1912. Rumsey Avenue, shown here, was named for Bronson Rumsey, one of the town founders. This view from near the corner of Thirteenth Street looks west towards Cedar (left) and Rattlesnake Mountains. (Now image, author.)

Waples Hospital, located on Rumsey Avenue between Thirteenth and Fourteenth Streets, was built in 1905 for $800. When Dr. F. A. Waples left Cody, it was renamed Cody General Hospital. With the opening of the newer and larger W. R. Coe Hospital in 1946, there was no longer any need for this facility. Today the building houses several apartments. (Now image, Jennifer Houze.)

3170—STATE SENATOR SCHWOB'S RESIDENCE, CODY, WYO.

Jakie Schwoob, a Wyoming state senator from 1905 to 1913, built this house on the corner of Fourteenth Street and Rumsey Avenue. In 1913, when Wyoming decided to license automobiles, Schwoob obtained statewide plate No. 1, as was befitting his position as president of the senate. He retained this number even after the state went to a county numbering system in 1929, as did his widow after his death. This house burned down many years later, when the Hindman family owned it. (Then image, Wyoming State Archives, State Parks and Cultural Resources; now image, author.)

The Beck house faced Eleventh Street and was built by Daisy Sorrenson Beck and George T. Beck in about 1909. Daisy taught school in the community of Marquette, west of Cody, before working as Beck's secretary at the Shoshone Irrigation Company. Their house became the social center of the town for many years, and longtime residents have fond memories of attending parties there. In 1966, new owners tore the house down in order to build the Manor, a senior citizen apartment complex. (Then image, PCA, 86-001-011; now image, author.)

Across the street to the north from where the Beck house once stood is the home built by sheep rancher Reuben C. Hargraves. The ranch was north of Cody, but as was common with sheep ranchers, they lived in town, so this was Hargraves's primary residence. The man pictured holding the horse is believed to be Hargraves, as his hobby was raising harness racehorses. The people in the background are unidentified. (Then image, PCA, 95-180-176; now image, Jennifer Houze.)

This house is located on the corner of Tenth Street and Bleistein Avenue. Louis "L. R." Ewart began construction on the house in 1910 and completed it in 1912. He was president of the First National Bank of Cody and was active in the Cody Club, predecessor to the current Cody Chamber of Commerce. After serving two terms in the Wyoming State Legislature, he was elected Speaker of the House during his last term from 1920 through 1921. Sitting on the front steps in about 1918 are, from left to right, Dorothy, Erwin, and Keene Ewart, children of Louis and Gertrude. (Then image, John Kappler collection; now image, Jennifer Houze.)

Frank Houx, Cody's first mayor (1901–1902 and 1906–1910), was the original owner of this house built in 1909 by Algott Johnson. Houx was also governor of Wyoming from 1917 through 1919. The Walter Kepford family bought the house in 1916, and they can be seen in the car, though individually they cannot be identified. The house was moved from the corner of Sheridan Avenue and Eighth Street to Rumsey Avenue in 1996, where it is a bed-and-breakfast known as the Mayor's Inn. (Then image, Dale and Bill Delph collection; now image, author.)

The original fire hall for the Cody Volunteer Fire Department Hook and Ladder Company No. 1 was located several blocks from downtown. By 1909, the firefighters had been outfitted with slickers and helmets by Buffalo Bill. Some of the firefighters pictured are Dr. James Bradbury, Guss Holm, George Taylor, Andy Larson, Barney Cone, Walter Schwoob, Archie Abbott, Roy McGinnis, Carl Hammitt, Col. J. H. Peake, and Nick Noble. Today it is the Salsbury Avenue Inn, a bed-and-breakfast. (Then image, PCA, 88-07-002; now image, author.)

The Irma Hotel's barroom was a favorite gathering place for the men of Cody, especially when the colonel was in town. The elegant cherrywood bar was made in France, shipped across the Atlantic Ocean to New York City, traveled overland by train to Red Lodge, Montana, and then brought by wagon to Cody. It was installed in the barroom, now the main dining room, in time for the opening of the hotel in 1902. Standing at the bar in the vintage image, from left to right, are Cody, unidentified, the bartender, George T. Beck, and unidentified. The staff of the Irma decorates for all the main holidays, including Halloween, as seen in the modern photograph. (Then image, PCA, P95-75-107; now image, author.)

With the arrival of the railroad (1901) and the completion of the Shoshone Dam (1910), which improved irrigation and made ranching and farming more attractive, the town grew in population and area. Park County was created from Big Horn County in 1909, and Cody was named the county seat. This view overlooking Cody is from the hill near Thirteenth Street, known by old-timers as "Taggart Hill," in about 1912. Heart Mountain is in the distance, and the Irma Hotel is on the left in the vintage photograph, though hidden by trees now as seen in the modern image. (Then image, American Heritage Center, University of Wyoming; now image, author.)

THE ORIGINAL TOWN

SCHOOLS, CHURCHES, AND PUBLIC BUILDINGS

The Little Red School was the only school in Cody in the early years. It housed grades 1 through 12 and was built in two stages. The wooden section (left) was built in 1904, and the larger brick part (right) was constructed in 1909. In 1922, a new high school was built to the north of the Little Red School to ease crowding. (Author's collection.)

Dr. Mark Chamberlin, a dentist, and his wife, Agnes, built the Hotel Chamberlin in 1904, and they took in boarders rather than overnight guests. The dentist's office was next door on the north side of the hotel. Agnes worked for the town's newspaper, the *Cody Enterprise,* and later as secretary for the Cody Club, the forerunner to the chamber of commerce. In 2005 and 2006, the building was renovated by Susan and Ev Diehl and is doing business as the Chamberlin Inn. (Then image, Chamberlin Inn collection; now image, author.)

SCHOOLS. CHURCHES, AND PUBLIC BUILDINGS

The First National Bank constructed this building at the corner of Thirteenth Street and Sheridan Avenue in 1912. Previously the bank had been in the Walls Building located one block west on the north side of the street. In 1958, this bank merged with the Shoshone Bank and moved directly across the street to the north. Cody Drug then occupied this building from 1959 to 1989. (Then image, PCA, P94-26-04; now image, author.)

The Cody Hotel was the first hotel in Cody. Built in 1896, it primarily took in boarders. It was torn down in the mid-1960s. Until recently, when the menu board was erected on the side of the Silver Dollar Bar, the roof outline could be seen on the wall where it had butted up against the bar. (Then image, Sturm/Lovelace collection; now image, author.)

SCHOOLS, CHURCHES, AND PUBLIC BUILDINGS

The Masonic Temple was still under construction in 1912 when a "Cody Zephyr"—a local term for Cody's strong winds—came through and blew down sections of several walls. While most of the damage has been repaired by the time this photograph was taken, it was extensive enough that the building was not completed until 1915. Notice that the ledge over the doorway has not been replaced yet, nor has the cornerstone been placed on the lower right side of the front wall. (Then image, PCA, 95-62.60; now image, author.)

The first Christ Episcopal Church was built in 1902 as the result of a winning hand in a poker game. Held at Tom Purcell's saloon, the participants were Col. William F. Cody, George Beck, Purcell, and two ranchers from Meeteetse. When the pot reached $550, which was considered too much for one man, the winner agreed to donate the funds to build a church of his choice. Beck won, and the "Poker Church" was built for $2,000. (Then image, PCA, 89P-23.5; now image, Jennifer Houze.)

SCHOOLS, CHURCHES, AND PUBLIC BUILDINGS

Cody's Carnegie Library was built in 1916 to replace the smaller stone one that had been built with funds raised by the Women's Club of Cody in 1906. From 1943 to 1969, Margaret Murray Martin was the head librarian, and she is still remembered by many longtime Cody residents. In 1963, the Carnegie Library was deemed too small, so it was torn down and a new building (as seen in the modern image) was erected facing Eleventh Street. In 2008, the fourth Cody Library opened in the Park County Complex located on Heart Mountain Street, leaving the former library building vacant. (Then image, Sturm/Lovelace collection; now image, author.)

When the Wyoming State Legislature authorized the formation of Park County from Big Horn County in 1909, Cody became the county seat. The first county office structure, known as the Spencer Building, was soon too crowded, so in 1912 construction of this facility began on land that was reserved for a city park. Overcrowding became an issue again in the late 1970s, but due to public protest against demolishing the 1912 courthouse, the new building became an addition to the original in 1984. This created an unusual configuration between the two buildings, as the floors do not match up. (Then image, PCA, 86-8.9; now image, author.)

First Term of Court held in Park Co.

According to the notation at the bottom of this photograph, it was taken in 1912 during the first term of court held on the second floor of the new courthouse. The presiding judge is Percy W. Metz, and the only other identifiable person is seated in the center of the courtroom with his arm resting on the back of his chair, lawyer William "Billy" Simpson. The Simpson family is well known throughout the state of Wyoming for their political and civic service, including Simpson's grandsons Peter and Alan. (Then image, PCA, P06-26-11; now image, author.)

Organized in 1905, the First Presbyterian Church began construction on this building in 1910. Located at the northeast corner of Beck Avenue and Eleventh Street, the church had a beautiful stained-glass window given by Colonel Cody and two of his sisters in memory of their parents, Mary and Isaac Cody. The congregation outgrew this building, and there was no room to expand at this site, so a new church was built on Twenty-third Street in 1968. The Cody window was brought from the first church and installed in the parlor of the new building. (Then image, Sturm/Lovelace collection; now image, author.)

SCHOOLS. CHURCHES, AND PUBLIC BUILDINGS

"Badland" Dave McFall built the Hart Mountain Inn in about 1898. Why he had that nickname is not known, other than the presumption that he came from the badlands. The hotel was a favorite of ranchers and farmers when they came to town for supplies and had to spend the night in Cody. The spelling of Heart Mountain was in dispute in the early years of the town but is now usually spelled "Heart." When this building was restored, the owners retained the historical "Hart" spelling. (Then image, PCA, P00-06-040; now image, author.)

The Cody Post Office was built in 1927 and remained here until 1982, when the need for a larger facility necessitated its move up the nearby hill to Stampede Avenue. It was the town's meeting place each morning, a social event that was lost after the move. It now houses businesses and offices but still retains much of its original interior decorative features. (Now image, Jennifer Houze.)

The Methodist Church organized on January 18, 1902, and built its church on Beck Avenue and Sixteenth Street. It was dedicated that same year in the fall with Rev. E. P. Hughes as the first minister. Today this is a bed-and-breakfast called Sage Brush Art Studio, and the current Methodist Church is across the street. (Then image, PCA, 89P-42.88; now image, Jennifer Houze.)

With Cody's population growing, the need for a high school became evident. This school was dedicated in February 1922 and was used until 1953 when another building was erected. Eventually this front section became Cody Junior High until 1994 when the school district adopted a middle school system of grades six through eight, resulting in the construction of the Cody Middle School on the east side of town. (Then image, Sturm/Lovelace collection; now image, author.)

SCHOOLS, CHURCHES, AND PUBLIC BUILDINGS

CHAPTER 3

OUTLYING AREAS

The Burlington Inn, or Cody Inn, was built in 1922 to accommodate tourists arriving by train. It had over 90 rooms and a dining room that seated between 400 and 500 people. In the early 1950s, part of the hotel was torn down, and the Husky Oil Company moved the rest a little east for its offices. (Sturm/Lovelace collection.)

E. M. Westerveld—of the Land and Industrial Commission for the Chicago, Burlington and Quincy Railroad—stands on the track just east of the Cody Depot and the Burlington Inn. While many in the town wanted the railroad line to continue on west to Yellowstone National Park, the Burlington and Quincy apparently had no interest in doing so, thus, the tracks did not go past Cody. The water tower, seen in both photographs, was torn down in September 2010. (Then image, Wyoming State Archives, State Parks and Cultural Resources; now image, Jennifer Houze.)

Looking west towards Shoshone Canyon, Rattlesnake Mountain is on the right and Cedar Mountain is on the left. The road on the right in the modern image led from the Cody depot on the north side of the Shoshone River to the canyon and on to Shoshone Reservoir. A quick glance at both photographs seems to indicate that not much has changed since 1908, when the vintage photograph was taken. However, by looking closely at the background area, buildings can be seen. (Now image, Jennifer Houze.)

Agnes Chamberlin, owner of the Chamberlin Inn, deeded land for the Cody Airport to the town in December 1940. In 1947, Challenger Airlines (later Frontier Airlines) began the first regular passenger service to Cody, and night flights began seven years later. The first terminal, seen in the vintage photograph, was built in 1962 and remodeled in the 1990s. A brand-new terminal opened on December 7, 2010. (Then image, Sturm/Lovelace collection; now image, author.)

Charles DeMaris bought DeMaris Hot Springs on the Shoshone River about two miles west of Cody around 1883. A longtime favorite of Indians and locals for its healing benefits from the mineral springs, William F. Cody wanted to establish the town at this site for just that reason. DeMaris would not sell his land to Cody, and by 1895 he was developing the area into a health spa complete with a hotel and a pool in the river, and he had plans to bottle the spring water and market it for sale. From top to bottom in the vintage image are the pool house, the original bathhouse, and the hotel. Today this area is in private hands. (Then image, Wyoming State Archives, State Parks and Cultural Resources; now image, author.)

Irma Flat School is located approximately nine miles southwest of Cody in the area known as the Southfork, short for Southfork of the Shoshone River. It was active as a school from 1905 to 1942, with students in grades one through eight. The students would then go on to high school in town. The original photograph was taken some time between 1911 and 1914. It is now the home of the Irma Flat Mothers' Club. (Then image, PCA, P86-014-09; now image, author.)

Castle Rock (left) is a volcanic plug located in the Southfork about 20 miles from Cody. It is also known as Colter's Rock because it is thought that John Colter passed by it in the winter of 1807–1808 when he explored this area. While the Southfork area has seen many new homes and ranches in the past 20 or 30 years, that growth is not very visible here. (Then image, Len Pearson collection; now image, author.)

Buffalo Bill purchased this Southfork ranch from Bob Burns in 1895 and named it the TE after the brand on the cattle he purchased from his good friend Mike Russell of Deadwood, South Dakota. TE possibly stands for Trails End, although no one really knows for sure. He is seen in the vintage photograph sitting on the side of the well and holding the reins of his horse. Of all of his properties in Cody, the TE was his favorite. Here he could get away from the hectic pace of travel and show business to be a rancher and a family man. The ranch is privately owned now but still retains the TE name. (Then image, BBHC, P.69.293; now image, author.)

CHAPTER 4

GROWTH
AND EXPANSION

Looking west, the growth of Cody can be seen in this 1930s aerial image. No longer a town with only four streets running east to west, it actually had four blocks of Sheridan Avenue paved by then, and the population was about 1,800. The rodeo grounds, seen in the lower right-hand corner, were at this site until 1946. (BBHC, Mr. and Mrs. Charles Belden, PN.67.805.)

The Buffalo Bill Campgrounds were located on the northeast corner of Sixteenth Street and Sheridan Avenue and at the intersection of the only road out of town to the north and to Billings, Montana. Today it is still the only road leading to Billings directly from Cody. Behind this sign and a little left is the Holiday Inn, just one of several other accommodations that are part of this complex. (Then image, BBHC, P.5.1462; now image, author.)

GROWTH AND EXPANSION

Until recently, the corner across the street to the west from the campgrounds has been occupied by a gas station since 1938 when Husky Oil Company built one there. In 1979, a Canadian firm bought the company, but the station continued to be owned by Husky until at least 1982. Walgreens bought approximately two-thirds of the block and opened its store in 2009. (Then image, Wyoming State Archives, State Parks and Cultural Resources; now image, Jennifer Houze.)

GROWTH AND EXPANSION

As a tourist town, Cody has always been aware of the needs of its visitors, which means gas stations, places to eat, and places to stay. This Texaco station predates the Husky station on the other end of the same block. Notice the car on the lift outside the station in the vintage image. (Then image, Sturm/Lovelace collection; now image, author.)

Will Richard was a guide and an outfitter in addition to being a taxidermist. His Cody Museum housed a display of mounted heads and horns from around the region, as well as some from Africa, and also highlighted his work both as a hunter and as a taxidermist. Wendy's opened in Cody in 1982. (Then image, PCA, P97-28.03; now image, author.)

Bud Webster bought the existing Chevrolet dealership in 1937. It was located on the north side of Sheridan Avenue in the middle of the block. Harley Kinkade was a participant in the 1948 Cody Stampede Parade with the wagon he used to take guests on his Kinkade Summer Trips between Cody and Cooke City, Montana. Kinkade is believed to be the man leaning on the rear of the horse; the others are unidentified. (Then image, Sturm/Lovelace collection; now image, author.)

GROWTH AND EXPANSION

To the west of Webster Chevrolet, on the corner, was the Ford dealership. When Dick Soll, the Ford dealer, moved his dealership to Twelfth Street in 1949, Webster bought that property and the building, easily doubling the size of the Chevrolet dealership. In 1987, Webster Chevrolet moved to the corner of Sheridan Avenue and Seventeenth Street (the Greybull Hill corner), and Shoshone First National Bank (now Wells Fargo) bought the property and erected this building. (Then image, Sturm/Lovelace collection; now image, author.)

In mid-September 1947, construction began on a Safeway store located directly behind the Irma Hotel on Twelfth Street and was finished later that year on December 26. In 1973, Hatch's Hallmark moved into this building for five years, followed by Jack's Sports and Hardware for 10 years or so. The large replica Winchester Commemorative rifle, sponsored in a Fourth of July Stampede Parade by the Winchester Company and Husky Oil, was put on the roof about 1978 by Jack Skates. (Then image, Sturm/Lovelace collection; now image, author.)

GROWTH AND EXPANSION

By the early 1950s, when this vintage photograph was taken, Cody's population approached 4,200, and businesses occupied most of the lots on Sheridan Avenue, the main street of town. The Irma Hotel was still the focal point of the town's life, with the local radio station KODI situated across the street and located next to the Cody Theatre. Within a two-block radius were the Cody Library, the post office, the Park County Court House, and numerous restaurants, all of which contributed to a thriving community. (Now image, author.)

On April 25, 1959, the world premiere of *Young Land* was held at the Cody Theatre. It seemed that the entire town turned out to see the stars of the movie, Patrick Wayne and Yvonne Craig. The theater is still here and now hosts a cowboy musical revue during the summer months and musical concerts and performances throughout the year. (Then image, Sturm/Lovelace collection; now image, author.)

GROWTH AND EXPANSION

This Sinclair gas station was west of the theater on the corner of Sheridan Avenue and Eleventh Street. Subsequently, a bike store and then a Daylight Donuts bakery occupied this site. In 1978, when the property was sold, the gas station was torn down, and Murray's Apothecary, a pharmacy and gift shop, replaced it. (Now image, Jennifer Houze.)

Green Gables Court was a small motel west of the Cody Library on Sheridan Avenue during the 1940s, 1950s, and 1960s. The postwar recovery enabled many Americans to travel to Yellowstone, and many came through Cody needing a place to stay. This was one of several motels built during that time period, and other motels have followed the Green Gables in this location. (Then image, Sturm/Lovelace collection; now image, author.)

GROWTH AND EXPANSION

Cody High School's gymnasium was fine for physical education classes, but there was not enough room for fans attending the sporting events. When Cody Auditorium was built by the city in 1941, the school district decided to rent it, beginning in 1946. Here the 1949 boy's basketball team is playing an unidentified opponent. The team included Louis "Jr." Kousoulos, Don Kurtz, Hal Lee, Bob Moore, and Al Simpson (captain and future U.S. senator). Today this building hosts everything from craft and design shows to wedding receptions and auctions (as seen in the modern photograph). (Then image, Sturm/Lovelace collection; now image, author.)

Within six weeks of William F. Cody's death, a group of residents met on the porch of the Irma Hotel and founded the Buffalo Bill Memorial Association. Additionally, they decided to establish a museum to honor Buffalo Bill's memory and to locate it here in Cody if possible. On July 4, 1927, the Buffalo Bill Museum opened with a large celebration, including local and state dignitaries and former Wild West performers from around the country. Today the Cody Chamber of Commerce, the Cody Country Art League, and the Cody Visitor's Center occupy this building. (Now image, Jennifer Houze.)

1191—Buffalo Bill Museum, Cody, Wyomin

The Whitney Gallery of Western Art opened in 1959 at the location seen here in the vintage image. Ten years later, the Buffalo Bill Museum joined it, and collectively they were referred to as the Buffalo Bill Historical Center. Another wing was added for the Plains Indian Museum in 1979, followed by the Cody Firearms Museum in 1991 and the Draper Museum of Natural History in 2002. Additionally, the McCracken Research Library began operations in 1980. (Now image, Jennifer Houze.)

Buffalo Bill—The Scout, by Gertrude Vanderbilt Whitney, depicts Cody following the trail of some horses (there are hoof prints set in the ground at the horse's feet). Whitney, a well-known New York sculptress, was commissioned to create a statue in Buffalo Bill's likeness. It was dedicated on July 4, 1924, Buffalo Bill's favorite holiday, with most of the town present. Whitney donated the land for the statue and the Historical Center. (Now image, author.)

GROWTH AND EXPANSION

Situated where the Cody Branch of the First National Bank of Powell is now, Katie and Claude Brown opened the Buffalo Bill Fur Salon in 1947. It continued there for 50 years, until Katie sold the business and the new owner moved it into the Sheridan Building for several years. Not only did the Browns sell furs, but Claude raised minks from 1928 to 1953 on his "Cody Fox Farm." (Then image, PCA, P09-42-97; now image, author.)

The Minter family came here from Pennsylvania and bought the Sunset Motel. Jim Minter (in the coat and tie) and Beulah Mullins (in the dress) are shown with the unidentified housekeeping staff on August 23, 1963. The Minters sold the Sunset Motel to Bill Garlow, the present owner, in 1984. (Then image, Bill Garlow collection; now image, author.)

Canyon Cafeteria, Cody, Wyoming

In June 1986, two years after Bill Garlow bought the Sunset Motel, he purchased the Canyon Cafeteria, which was located next to the motel to the south. The cafeteria was owned by Mel and Price McGee and was a favorite place to eat of the townspeople. After extensive remodeling, the Sunset House Restaurant had its grand opening in May 1987. (Then image, Bill Garlow collection; now image, author.)

With an improving economy and the end of World War II, Cody saw an increase in tourists on their way to and from Yellowstone National Park. Keystone Court consisted of many small, individual cabins. The motel concept as it is known today had not been fully developed but soon would be. Ponderosa Campground, which occupies the same area, has some cabins and tents but has many more recreational vehicle sites. (Then image, Sturm/Lovelace collection; now image, author.)

GROWTH AND EXPANSION

Another motor court, as they were sometimes called, which was just a short distance from the Keystone Court, was Allen's Court. It was on the west, or far side, of Sulphur Creek (a small tributary of the Shoshone River named for the high presence of the gas it contained) and faced Yellowstone Highway. In the early 1990s, Walmart built a store at this location but later moved farther west to build a super center. (Then image, Bill Davis collection; now image, author.)

ALLEN'S COURT, Cody, Wyoming

The Cody Rodeo Grounds moved from near present-day Eastside School and Circle Drive to Stampede Avenue in 1946. It remained at this third location until 1976, when it moved to the present site west of town on the Yellowstone Highway. Looking south, there is nothing but farmland, except for the Kinkade Dairy that is hidden in the trees in the middle of the photograph. Today this area includes, clockwise from left to right, the Park County Complex, the U.S. post office, the Riley Arena and Recreation Center, and Cody Canal Park. (Then image, BBHC, Jack Richard Collection, PN.89.17.3030.01; now image, Lee Hermann.)

After World War II, families began to move into newly opened subdivisions on the south bench above Cody. In fact, Cody's population increased by about 30 percent after the war. The Sunset Grocery was part of this growth when it was built in 1949 on Stampede Avenue and Eighteenth Street. Martha Nan (seen here) and Paul James bought the store from her brother in 1963 and operated it until 1976. Today the building is used by a day care center. (Then image, Martha Nan and Paul James collection; now image, author.)

Ethyl and Frank James built the Stockade Motel in 1949 with eight rooms; it was also their residence. It sits on the edge of the bench overlooking Cody, with Heart Mountain to the north. In 1963, the motel became the James's private residence only and in 1975 was purchased by their daughter Fran and her husband, Ken. They completely renovated it two years later. (Then image, Fran Swope collection; now image, author.)

CHAPTER

THE ROAD TO YELLOWSTONE

West of Cody a dam was built at the confluence of the two branches of the Shoshone River. The Shoshone Dam was completed in January 1910, but three years later the water in the reservoir had to be drained in order to make repairs to the dam. The community of Marquette had been located where the reservoir is now. (BBHC, Jack Richard Collection, P.89.88.)

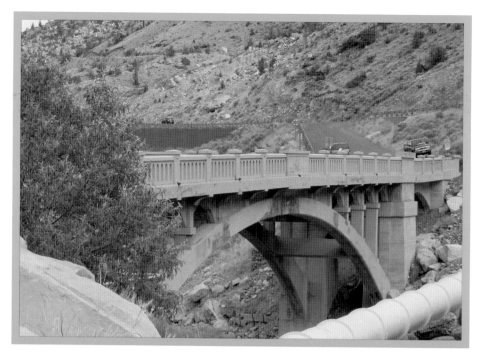

The Hayden Arch Bridge crosses the Shoshone River before Yellowstone Highway enters the steeper part of Shoshone Canyon. The bridge was completed on December 15, 1924, and is the only example of this type of bridge left in Park County. It is still in use to access fishing and the old road, but several decades ago the highway was straightened out and a new bridge was built over the river, bypassing the Hayden Arch Bridge. (Then image, Vaun Landgren collection; now image, author.)

THE ROAD TO YELLOWSTONE

PASSING THROUGH A TUNNEL ON CODY ROUTE TO YELLOWSTONE PARK.

A good portion of the original road through the canyon was built right along the river's edge. Work was started on the road prior to the construction of Shoshone Dam. It began in 1904 so that materials, construction equipment, and supplies could be transported over it to the work site. While blasting was done to start the tunnels, much of the work was done by hand with picks, shovels, and sledgehammers. Immigrants, for the most part, were hired to do the work. (Then image, Wyoming State Archives, State Parks and Cultural Resources; now image, author.)

The road was extremely narrow, even for the wagons and buggies of the time. In some places, there was enough room on the north side of the road to make "pullouts." These areas gave the wagons going up the hill the space to pull over to allow the downhill traffic to pass, as that traffic had the right-of-way. With little sunshine reaching the bottom of the canyon, the trip was cold and dangerous in the wintertime. (Then image, PCA, P00-04-16; now image, author.)

View in The Cody Pass.
Cody Road to Yellowstone.

Learning to drive up the narrow, steep dam hill was certainly a challenge for new drivers, as can be seen here, even though parts of the road were widened in the 1920s. However, it certainly became easier once the new road was built in 1959. Two of the three new tunnels can be seen almost directly above two of the older ones in the modern image. The steepest part of the canyon was yet to come for travelers. (Then image, PCA, P00-04-19; now image, Sturm/ Lovelace collection.)

The height of the Shoshone Dam was 325 feet when it was completed in 1910, and the observation area was reached by climbing down a long stairway seen here. It was the tallest dam in the country at that time. In the late 1980s, construction began to raise the dam another 25 feet, and it was completed in 1990. (Then image, Marge and Dick Wilder collection; now image, author.)

90. OBSERVATORY SUMMIT ON SHOSHONE DAM. ON THE CODY ROAD TO YELLOWSTONE PARK.

THE ROAD TO YELLOWSTONE

This view is looking west from the dam over the Shoshone Reservoir, where the community of Marquette had once been. Prior to filling the reservoir, most of the buildings had been moved away, and the residents had relocated elsewhere. When finished in 1910, the reservoir provided water to area farmers, ranchers, and home owners, in addition to being a recreational lake for boating, sailing, fishing, and even swimming. (Then image, Shoshone Irrigation District Archives, Powell, Wyoming; now image, author.)

The community of Wapiti, which is an Indian word for "elk," is located 20 miles west of Cody. When the road to Yellowstone was completed in 1903, it took wagons an entire day to make the trip from Cody. Once motorized travel became common, Wapiti could be reached by lunchtime. Until late December 2010, Wapiti Lodge (or its predecessor, the Green Lantern) housed the Wapiti Post Office since 1904, when its first postmaster was Clarence Woods. (Then image, PCA, P97-42.80; now image, author.)

When Marquette was flooded to create the reservoir, some families chose to relocate farther west to Wapiti, creating the need for a school. In 1910, this tent school was located a little to the north of the present one and nearer to the North Fork of the Shoshone River. A year later, a permanent school was built, which has been added on to several times over the years. From left to right are teacher June Hale Brundage, Vera Wagoner, Bill Leabold, Don Wagoner, Leonard Morris, and Herchall Green. (Then image, PCA; now image, author.)

President Benjamin Harrison designated the present-day Shoshone National Forest as the Yellowstone Timber Reserve in 1891, the first reserve in the country. The Wapiti Ranger Station, completed in 1905, was the country's first ranger station. Today there is a combination visitor's center and ranger station on the north side of the Yellowstone Highway, but the original station is still used for meetings and classes by the U.S. Forest Service. (Then image, Sturm/Lovelace; now image, author.)

Numerous volcanic rock formations can be seen on the trip from Cody to Yellowstone. Many of them were given names by the early tourists because they resemble animals, people, or geological features. It was undoubtedly a fun way to pass the time as people made their way through the valley. This is known as the Laughing Pig. (Then image, Sturm/Lovelace; now image, author.)

Farther along the road on the south side, and many rock formations later, Henry Ford can be seen driving his Model T. Camping, hiking, picnicking, and fishing are just some of the recreational activities to do while traveling to Yellowstone. It often seems as though the campgrounds are frequented more by Park County residents than by visitors to the area if the license plates on the cars in the parking lots are any indication. (Then image, Sturm/Lovelace; now image, author.)

Elephant Head Lodge, aptly named for a nearby rock formation (not visible), began first as a summer home in 1920, and became a guest ranch in 1926 owned by Josephine Goodman Thurston, daughter of Buffalo Bill's sister Julia. Josie's husband, Harry Thurston, was an early forest ranger who helped build the Wapiti Ranger Station in 1904 and 1905. The original lodge had space for only 20 guests. (Then image, PCA, P06-06-116; now image, author.)

Pahaska Tepee was Buffalo Bill's hunting lodge, located a little more than 50 miles from Cody and about two miles before the east gate of Yellowstone. He chose the site himself, blazing the trees with an ax to mark the exact desired location. It was completed in 1904. The colonel enjoyed bringing groups of friends here to hunt when he returned to Cody at the end of a long Wild West season. (Then image, PCA, P04-75-16; now image, author.)

The entrance to Yellowstone National Park from Cody was first known as the Sylvan Pass Ranger Station but is now referred to either as Eastgate or as the East Entrance, and it has an elevation of 6,951 feet. Automobiles were first allowed into the Park on August 1, 1915, and they had to share the roadways with horse traffic. By 1916, horses were no longer allowed on the park roads except those used by the military and subsequently the park rangers. Today over 400,000 vehicles pass through the gate annually, though it is only open to snowmobiles in the winter. (Then image, PCA, P99-37-126; now image, author.)

Two miles beyond the East Entrance is Sylvan Pass at an elevation of 8,541 feet. This increase in height from the entrance necessitated a "corkscrew bridge," a gradual, curving road that enabled traffic to slowly wind its way to the top of the pass. The first bridge was a wooden trestle type completed in 1904, a year after the road to Pahaska Tepee was finished. When automobiles were allowed into the park in 1915, it soon became apparent that a new bridge was necessary, as the amount of traffic had increased and was heavier. This concrete bridge was completed in 1919 and was in use for 10 years or so. Once a new road was built higher up on the side of the mountain in 1929, the corkscrew bridge was no longer necessary. (Then image, PCA, P80-6.05; now image, Walter F. Goodman Jr. collection.)

THE ROAD TO YELLOWSTONE

BIBLIOGRAPHY

Andren, Gladys. *Life Among Ladies By the Lake*. Cody, WY: self-published, 1984.

Barnhart, Bill. *The Northfork Trail*. Cody, WY: Elkhorn Publishing, 1982.

Bartlett, Richard A. *From Cody to the World*. Cody, WY: Buffalo Bill Historical Center, 1992.

Chamberlin, Agnes. *The Cody Club, 1900–1999*. Cody, WY: Cody Chamber of Commerce, 1999.

Churchill, Beryl, Jeannie Cook, and Jonita Monteith. *Challenging the Canyon*. Cody, WY: Wordsworth, 2001.

Cody Centennial Committee and the Park County Historical Society. *Cody Historic Walking Tour; centennial ed*. Cody, WY: self-published, 1996.

Cook, Jeannie, Lynn Johnson Houze, Bob Edgar, and Paul Fees. *Buffalo Bill's Town in the Rockies*. Virginia Beach, VA: Donning Company Publishers, 1996.

Frost, Dick. *Tracks, Trails, and Tails*. Cody, WY: self-published, 1984.

Hicks, Lucille P., ed. *The Park County Story*. Dallas, TX: Taylor Publishing Co., 1980.

Houze, Lynn Johnson. *Images Of America: Cody*. Charleston, SC: Arcadia Publishing, 2008.

Johansson-Murray, Ester. *A History of the North Fork of the Shoshone River*. Cody, WY: Lone Eagle Multi Media, 1996.

Kensel, W. Hudson. *Pahaska Tepee; Buffalo Bill's Old Hunting Lodge and Hotel, a History, 1901–1946*. Cody, WY: Buffalo Bill Historical Center, 1987.

Park County Travel Council. *2009 Annual Report*. Cody, WY: 2010.

Roberts, Phil, David Roberts, and Steve Roberts. *Wyoming Almanac*, fourth ed., rev. Laramie, WY: Sky West Press, 1996.

Wasden, David. *From Beaver to Oil*. Cheyenne, WY: Pioneer Printing and Stationery Co., 1973.

www.arcadiapublishing.com

Discover books about the town where you grew up, the cities where your friends and families live, the town where your parents met, or even that retirement spot you've been dreaming about. Our Web site provides history lovers with exclusive deals, advanced notification about new titles, e-mail alerts of author events, and much more.

MADE IN THE USA

Arcadia Publishing, the leading local history publisher in the United States, is committed to making history accessible and meaningful through publishing books that celebrate and preserve the heritage of America's people and places. Consistent with our mission to preserve history on a local level, this book was printed in South Carolina on American-made paper and manufactured entirely in the United States.

This book carries the accredited Forest Stewardship Council (FSC) label and is printed on 100 percent FSC-certified paper. Products carrying the FSC label are independently certified to assure consumers that they come from forests that are managed to meet the social, economic, and ecological needs of present and future generations.

FSC
Mixed Sources
Product group from well-managed forests and other controlled sources

Cert no. SW-COC-001530
www.fsc.org
© 1996 Forest Stewardship Council

Find Your Place in History.